COLORADO
reflections

PHOTOGRAPHY BY

John Fielder

WITH SELECTED QUOTATIONS

First frontispiece Scrub oak trees at sunset, Uncompahgre National Forest

Second frontispiece October aspen trees, Uncompahgre National Forest

Left Rocky Mountain National Park ponds

Above Stranded elk calf, Sam Capps Ranch, Huerfano County

JOHN FIELDER PUBLISHING

SILVERTHORNE, COLORADO

Most true happiness comes

from one's inner life,

from the disposition

of the mind and soul.

Admittedly, a good inner life

is difficult to achieve,

especially in these trying times.

It takes reflection and

contemplation and

self-discipline.

—WILLIAM L. SHIRER

Sunrise on Longs Peak at Chasm Lake, Rocky Mountain National Park

Canada Geese in Peanut Lake near Crested Butte
Left: Yampa River, Chuck Lewis State Wildlife Area near Steamboat Springs

Sunrise at Grant Ranch, Jefferson County

Sunrise on Mount Powell, Gore Range, Eagles Nest Wilderness

*Reflect upon your
present blessings—of which
every man has many—
not on your past misfortunes,
of which all men have some.*

—CHARLES DICKENS

Sunrise on East Spanish Peak, Sam Capps Ranch, Huerfano County

Paradise Divide, Gunnison National Forest

Sunrise at Last Dollar Ranch near Ridgway
Overleaf: Bull, cow, and calf moose along Highway 9, Summit County

Sunrise in Wild Basin, Rocky Mountain National Park

Sunrise on Hallett Peak from Lake Haiyaha, Rocky Mountain National Park

Always vote for principle,

though you may vote alone,

and you may cherish the

sweetest reflection that

your vote is never lost.

—JOHN QUINCY ADAMS

Mountain goat skull, Gore Range, Eagles Nest Wilderness

Sunset, Gore Range, Eagles Nest Wilderness

Gunnison River, Gunnison Gorge Wilderness

James M. Robb–Colorado River State Park at Island Acres, Mesa County
Right: Ohio Creek, Gunnison County

Coneflowers, Hartong Ranch, Archuleta County

My role in society,

or any artist's or poet's role,

is to try and express

what we all feel.

Not to tell people how

to feel. Not as a preacher,

not as a leader, but

as a reflection of us all.

—JOHN LENNON

Sunrise, Gore Range, Eagles Nest Wilderness
Right: Sunset on Mount Yale, Collegiate Peaks Wilderness
Overleaf: Autumn along the Gunnison River, Gunnison County

Wilson Peak, Wilson Mesa near Telluride

Willow Creek, Arapaho National Forest

Both: Sunrise at Peanut Lake, Crested Butte

*Our observation of
nature must be diligent,
our reflection profound,
and our experiments exact.
We rarely see these
three means combined;
and for this reason,
creative geniuses are
not common.*

—DENIS DIDEROT

Sunset at Paradise Divide, Gunnison National Forest

Sunrise, Gore Range, Eagles Nest Wilderness

Sunrise, Gore Range, Eagles Nest Wilderness

Molas Lake, San Juan National Forest

Spring at Parkview Mountain Ranch, Jackson County
Overleaf: Sunset at Paradise Divide, Gunnison National Forest

The world is a looking glass,

and gives back to every man

the reflection of his own face.

Frown at it and it will in

turn look sourly upon you;

laugh at it and with it, and

it is a jolly kind companion.

—WILLIAM MAKEPEACE THACKERAY

Sunrise at Yust Ranch, Colorado River, Grand County

Black bear, Sam Capps Ranch, Huerfano County

Smith Fork of the Gunnison River, Sunrise Canyon Ranch, Montrose County

Pidgeon and Turret Peaks, Needle Mountains, Weminuche Wilderness

Upper Avalanche Creek, Maroon Bells-Snowmass Wilderness
Overleaf: Sunrise at Peanut Lake, Crested Butte

Childhood is not only the childhood we really had but also the impressions we formed of it in our adolescence and maturity. That is why childhood seems so long. Probably every period of life is multiplied by our reflections upon the next.

—CESARE PAVESE

Gunnison River, Gunnison Gorge Wilderness

El Rancho Pinoso along Rio Blanco, Archuleta County

Rusk Ranch, Sangre de Cristo Mountains, Custer County
Overleaf: Colorado River, Grand County

Woods Lake, Uncompahgre National Forest

What is government itself

but the greatest of all reflections

on human nature? If men were angels,

no government would be necessary.

If angels were to govern men,

neither external nor internal

controls on government would

be necessary.

—JAMES MADISON

Sunrise, Needle Mountains, Weminuche Wilderness
Right: Morning twilight, Wild Basin, Rocky Mountain National Park

Castle Pines Golf Club, Douglas County

Little Snake River, Focus Ranch, Routt County

ISBN: 978-0-9832769-1-3

PHOTOGRAPHS AND TEXT:
Copyright John Fielder 2011.
All rights reserved.

PUBLISHED BY:
John Fielder Publishing
P.O. Box 26890
Silverthorne, Colorado 80497

PRINTED IN China

EDITOR:
Deb Olson

GRAPHIC DESIGN:
Rebecca Finkel, F + P Graphic Design

FRONT COVER PHOTOGRAPH:
Sunset, Holy Cross Wilderness

BACK COVER PHOTOGRAPH:
Lake Fork of the Gunnison River,
Rivergate Ranch, Gunnison County

For information about all of John
Fielder's books and calendars, galleries,
speaking engagements and book
signings, and workshops visit
www.johnfielder.com. Book retailers
contact derek@imprintgroupwest.com
to purchase inventory.

John Fielder Photography Workshops

Learn landscape photography directly from John Fielder in Colorado's most scenic locales, at his annual Autumn in Colorado workshop. Find out how John creates his award-winning images and gain a deeper understanding of the visual aspects of nature in comprehensive classroom sessions and at field shoots in John's favorite locations. Learn how to spot photo opportunities, experiment with different perspectives, improve compositions and get an insider's look at professional techniques. We use digital cameras only and bring our laptop computers for constructive critiques. Appropriate for practiced beginner and intermediate photographers, workshop programs are designed to help students reach at least their next level of ability. Enrollment is limited to ensure the highest quality experience. Most workshops are conducted with the assistance of a second professional landscape photographer so that everyone enjoys personal attention and no question is left unanswered. Visit **www.johnfielder.com** for complete information on this and other photography workshops.